Guitar Solos and Duets

Alfred's
INSTRUMENTAL PLAY-ALONG
mp3

TnT²
CUSTOM MIX

M000106225

THE HOBBIT
AN UNEXPECTED JOURNEY
INSTRUMENTAL SOLOS

Music Composed by
HOWARD SHORE

For instructions on accessing the MP3s, TNT 2 software, and piano accompaniment PDFs on the DVD-ROM, turn to the inside back cover.

Arranged by Bill Galliford and Ethan Neuburg
Orchestral recording produced by Dan Warner, Doug Emery and Lee Levin
Guitars arranged and recorded by Aaron Stang

Alfred

Music Land
200 Gateway Dr.
Bel Air, MD 21014-4200

ISBN 10: 0-7390-9601-X
ISBN-13: 978-0-7390-9601-7

Track 1: Demo
Track 2: Play-Along

MY DEAR FRODO

Lyrics by
PHILIPPA BOYENS

Music by
HOWARD SHORE

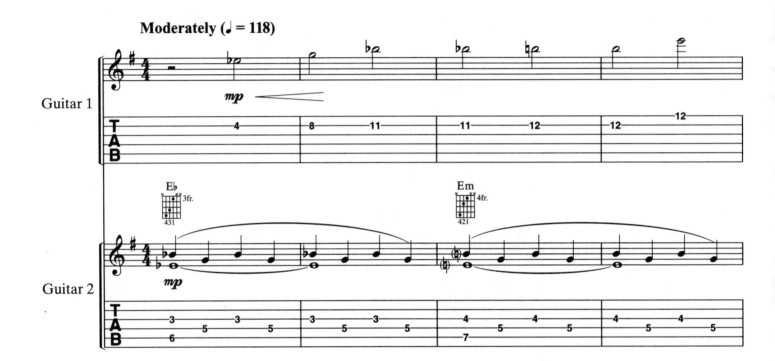

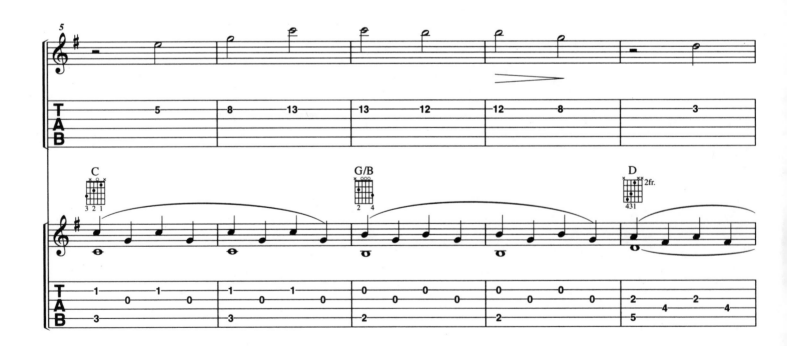

Axe or Sword? - 6 - 6

THE ADVENTURE BEGINS

Track 7: Demo
Track 8: Play-Along

Music by
HOWARD SHORE

Moderately bright (♩ = 156)

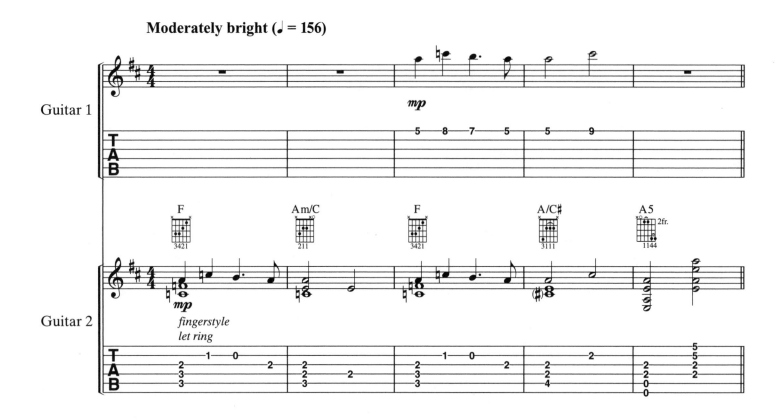

The Adventure Begins - 3 - 1

The Adventure Begins - 3 - 3

WARG-SCOUTS

Track 9: Demo
Track 10: Play-Along

Music by
HOWARD SHORE

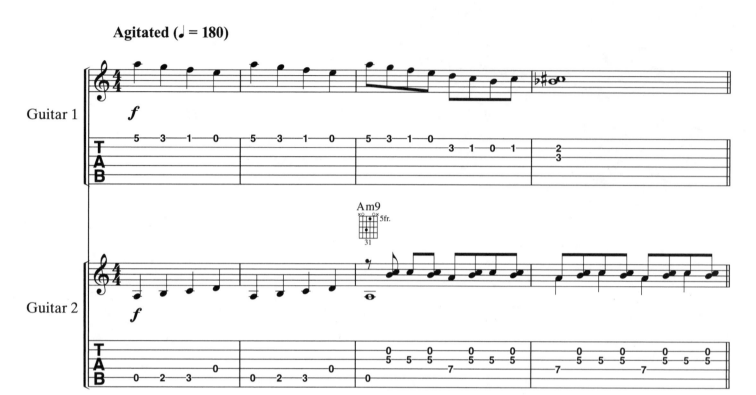

Warg-Scouts - 8 - 1

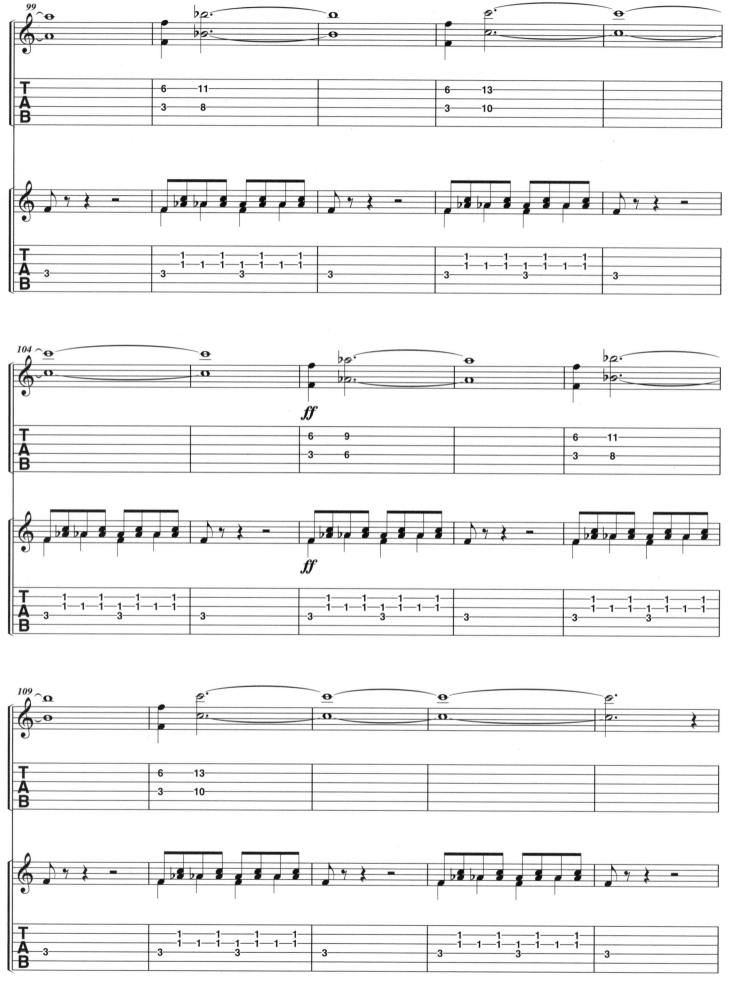

Track 11: Demo
Track 12: Play-Along

A GOOD OMEN

Lyrics by J.R.R. TOLKIEN
Adapted by PHILIPPA BOYENS

Music by
HOWARD SHORE

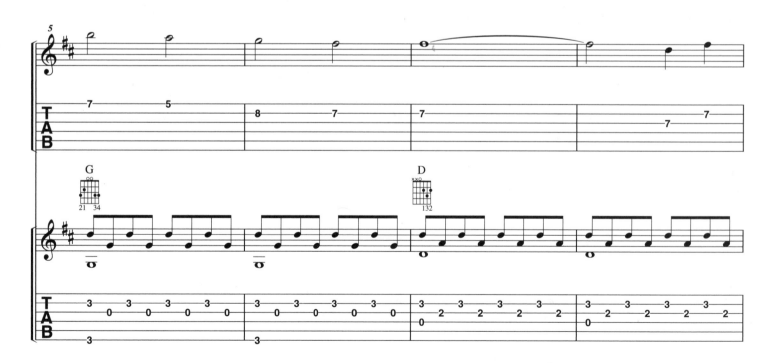

A Good Omen - 7 - 1

A Good Omen - 7 - 6

SONG OF THE LONELY MOUNTAIN

Lyrics by
NEIL FINN

Music Composed by
NEIL FINN, DAVID DONALDSON,
DAVID LONG, STEVE ROCHE
and JANET RODDICK

Note: To match recording, or to perform with
the matching string arrangements, Capo II

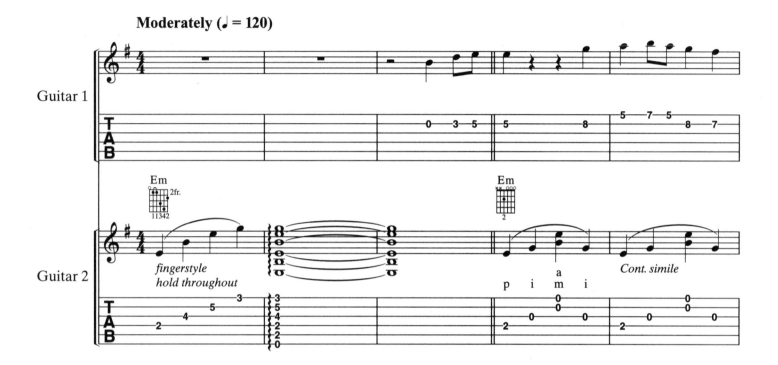

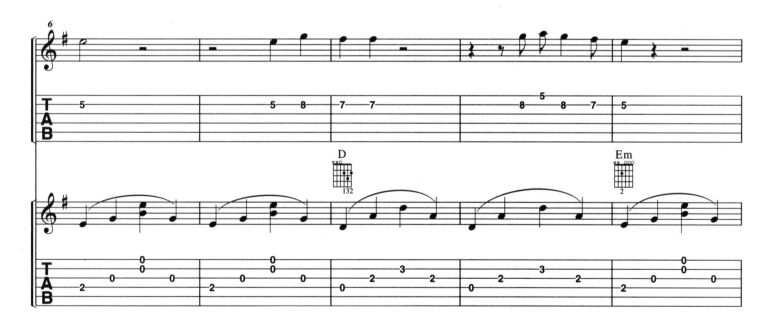

Song of the Lonely Mountain - 7 - 1

Song of the Lonely Mountain - 7 - 2

44

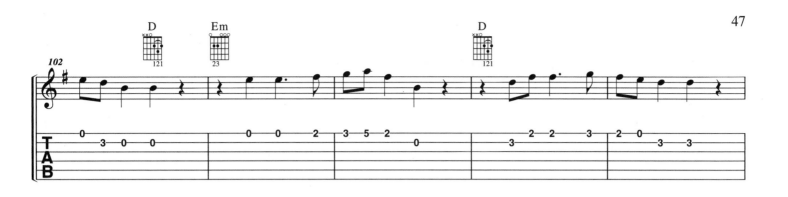

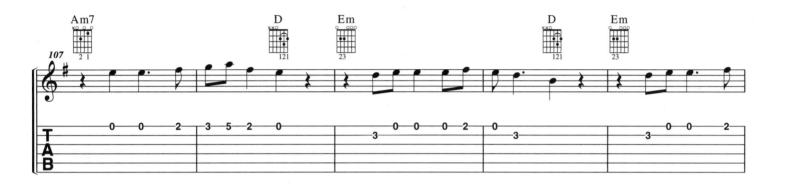

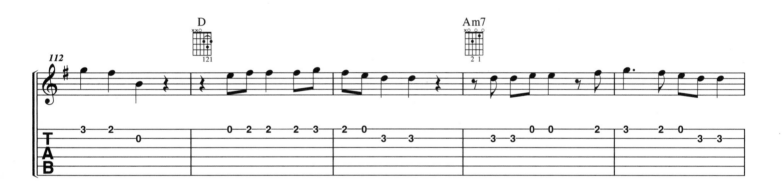

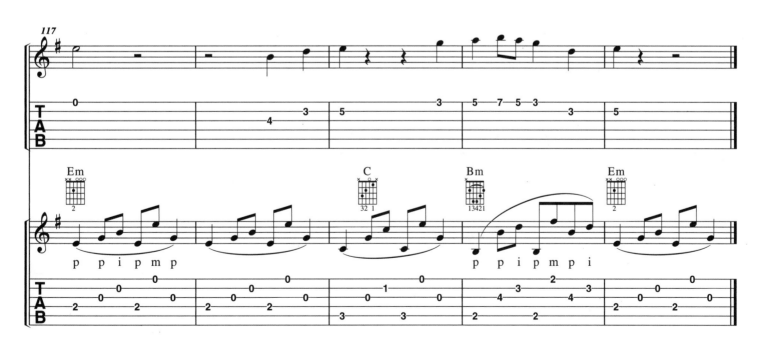

Song of the Lonely Mountain - 7 - 7

DREAMING OF BAG END

Track 15: Demo
Track 16: Play-Along

Music by
HOWARD SHORE

To match recorded key, Capo II

Moderately (♩ = 96)

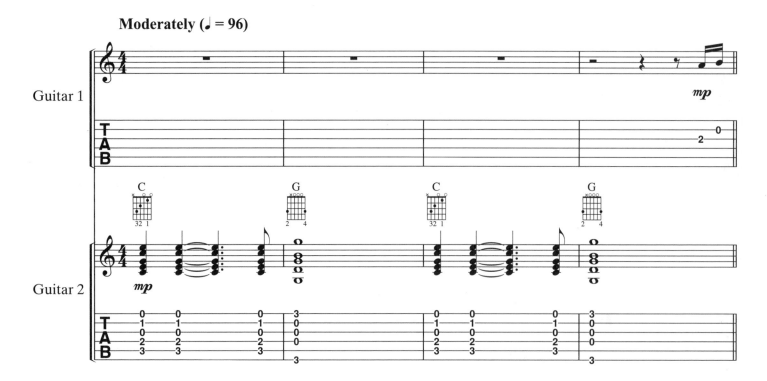

Guitar 1

Guitar 2

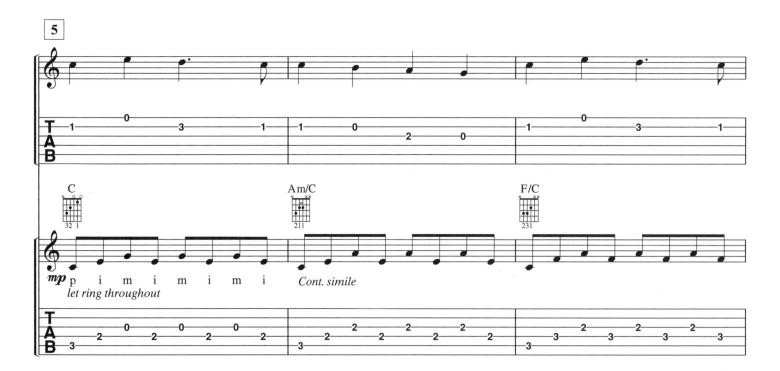

let ring throughout

Cont. simile

Dreaming of Bag End - 4 - 1

50

Dreaming of Bag End - 4 - 3

A VERY RESPECTABLE HOBBIT

Track 17: Demo
Track 18: Play-Along

Music by
HOWARD SHORE

Moderately (♩ = 120)

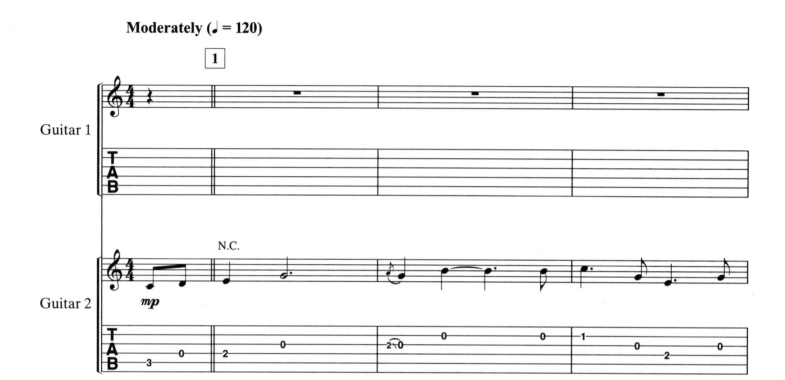

Guitar 1

Guitar 2

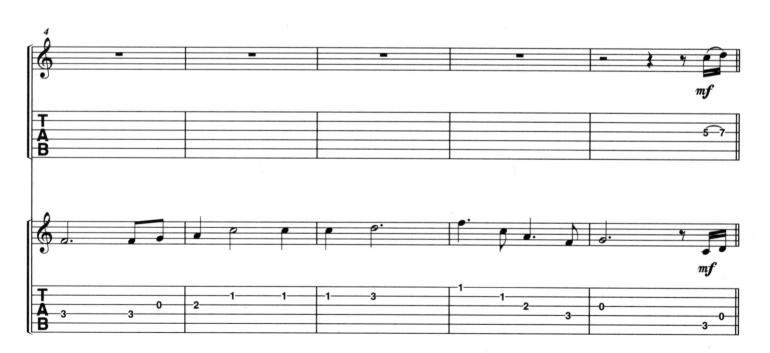

A Very Respectable Hobbit - 4 - 1

24 **A little slower (♩ = 120)**

Note: To match recording, or to perform with the matching string arrangements, Capo V

EREBOR

Music by
HOWARD SHORE

Track 19: Demo
Track 20: Play-Along

Erebor - 3 - 1

Erebor - 3 - 2

58

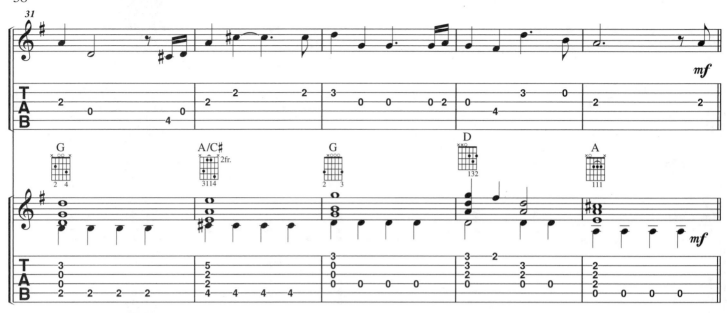

Erebor - 3 - 3

THE DWARF LORDS

Music by
HOWARD SHORE

Moderately (♩ = 104)

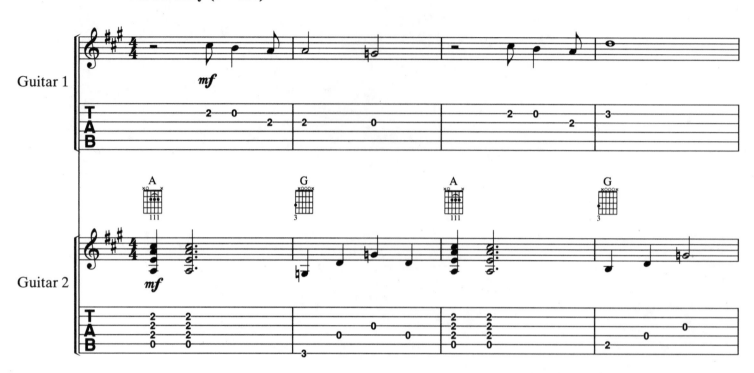

The Dwarf Lords - 4 - 1

17 Slower (♩ = 92)

62

The Dwarf Lords - 4 - 3

The Dwarf Lords - 4 - 4

TABLATURE EXPLANATION
TAB illustrates the six strings of the guitar.
Notes and chords are indicated by the placement of fret numbers on each string.

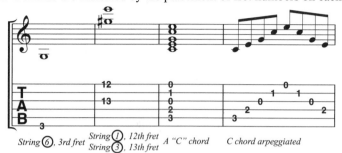

String ⑥, 3rd fret   String ①, 12th fret   A "C" chord   C chord arpeggiated
            String ③, 13th fret

BENDING NOTES

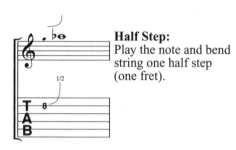

Half Step:
Play the note and bend string one half step (one fret).

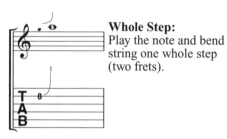

Whole Step:
Play the note and bend string one whole step (two frets).

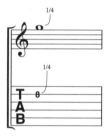

Slight Bend/ Quarter-Tone Bend:
Play the note and bend string sharp.

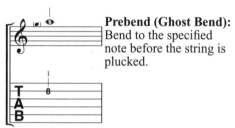

Prebend (Ghost Bend):
Bend to the specified note before the string is plucked.

Prebend and Release:
Play the already-bent string, then immediately drop it down to the fretted note.

Unison Bend:
Play both notes and immediately bend the lower note to the same pitch as the higher note.

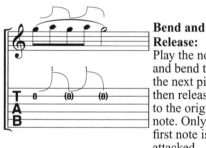

Bend and Release:
Play the note and bend to the next pitch, then release to the original note. Only the first note is attacked.

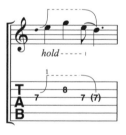

Bends Involving More Than One String:
Play the note and bend the string while playing an additional note on another string. Upon release, relieve the pressure from the additional note allowing the original note to sound alone.

Bends Involving Stationary Notes:
Play both notes and immediately bend the lower note up to pitch. Release bend as indicated.

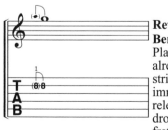

Reverse Bend:
Play the already bent string, then immediately release to drop pitch to fretted note.

Unison Bend:
Play both notes and immediately bend the lower note to the same pitch as the higher note.

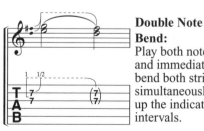

Double Note Bend:
Play both notes and immediately bend both strings simultaneously up the indicated intervals.

ARTICULATIONS

Hammer On (Ascending Slur): Play the lower note, then "hammer" your finger to the higher note. Only the first note is plucked.

Pull Off (Descending Slur): Play the higher note with your first finger already in position on the lower note. Pull your finger off the first note with a strong downward motion that plucks the string—sounding the lower note.

Legato Slide: Play the first note and, keeping pressure applied on the string, slide up to the second note. The diagonal line shows that it is a slide and not a hammer-on or a pull-off.

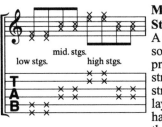

low stgs.   mid. stgs.   high stgs.

Muted Strings: A percussive sound is produced by striking the strings while laying the fret hand across them.

P.M. - - - - - - ⌐

Palm Mute: The notes are muted (muffled) by placing the palm of the pick hand lightly on the strings, just in front of the bridge.

Left Hand Hammer: Using only the left hand, hammer on the first note played on each string.

Glissando: Play note and slide in specified direction.

hold - - - ⌐

Bend and Tap Technique: Play note and bend to specified interval. While holding bend, tap onto fret indicated with a "t."

Fretboard Tapping: Tap onto the note indicated by the "t" with a finger of the pick hand, then pull off to the following note held by the fret hand.

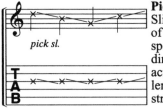

pick sl.

Pick Slide: Slide the edge of the pick in specified direction across the length of the strings.

trem. pick

Tremolo Picking: The note or notes are picked as fast as possible.

Trill: Hammer on and pull off consecutively and as fast as possible between the original note and the grace note.

Vibrato: The pitch of a note is varied by a rapid shaking of the fret-hand finger, wrist, and forearm.

Accent: Notes or chords are to be played with added emphasis.

Staccato (Detached Notes): Notes or chords are to be played about half their noted value and with separation.

HARMONICS

Natural Harmonic: A finger of the fret hand lightly touches the string at the note indicated in the TAB and is plucked by the pick producing a bell-like sound called a harmonic.

Artificial Harmonic: Fret the note at the first TAB number, lightly touch the string at the fret indicated in parens (usually 12 frets higher than the fretted note), then pluck the string with an available finger or your pick.

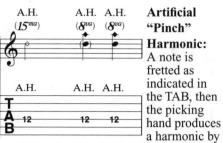

Artificial "Pinch" Harmonic: A note is fretted as indicated in the TAB, then the picking hand produces a harmonic by squeezing the pick firmly while using the tip of the index finger in the pick attack. If parenthesis are found around the fretted note, it does not sound. No parenthesis means both the fretted note and the A.H. are heard simultaneously.

RHYTHM SLASHES

Strum Marks/ Rhythm Slashes: Strum with the indicated rhythm pattern. Strum marks can be located above the staff or within the staff.

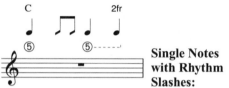

Single Notes with Rhythm Slashes: Sometimes single notes are incorporated into a strum pattern. The circled number below is the string and the fret number is above.

TREMOLO BAR

Specified Interval: The pitch of a note or chord is lowered to the specified interval and then return as indicated. The action of the tremolo bar is graphically represented by the peaks and valleys of the diagram.

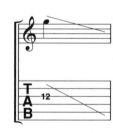

Unspecified Interval: The pitch of a note or chord is lowered, usually very dramatically, until the pitch of the string becomes indeterminate.

PICK DIRECTION

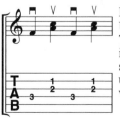

Downstrokes and Upstrokes: The downstroke is indicated with this symbol (∏) and the upstroke is indicated with this (V).